IMMA Series (4)

Irish Museum of Modern Art

Robin Marchesi

Barry Flanagan
Poet of the Building Site

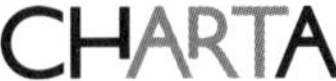

Editor
Christina Kennedy, Senior Curator: Head
of Collections
Johanne Mullan, National Programmer;
Collections

Design
Daniela Meda

Editorial Coordination
Filomena Moscatelli

Copyediting
Emily Ligniti

Copywriting and Press Office
Silvia Palombi

International Editorial Director
Francesca Sorace

Promotion and Web
Monica D'Emidio

Distribution
Anna Visaggi

Administration
Grazia De Giosa

Warehouse and Outlet
Roberto Curiale

Cover
Untitled, 1985, ceramic (five ceramic bowls),
dimensions variable
Collection Irish Museum of Modern Art,
Donation, Hester Van Roijen, 2006

Photo Credits
Denis Mortell; Dirk Pauwels; Donal Murphy;
Prudence Cuming Associates

Irish Museum of Modern Art
Áras Nua-Ealaíne na h-Éireann
Royal Hospital, Military Road
Kilmainham, Dublin 8
Ireland
Tel + 353-1-612-9900
Fax + 353-1-612-9999
e-mail: info@imma.ie • www.imma.ie

Edizioni Charta srl
Milano
via della Moscova, 27 - 20121
Tel. +39-026598098/026598200
Fax +39-026598577
e-mail: charta@chartaartbooks.it

Charta Books Ltd.
New York City
Tel. +1-313-406-8468
e-mail: international@chartaartbooks.it

www.chartaartbooks.it

Director
Enrique Juncosa

Collections Department

Senior Curator: Head of Collections
Christina Kennedy

National Programmer
Johanne Mullan

Assistant Curator: Collections
Marguerite O'Molloy

Assistant Curator: Collections
Georgie Thompson

Collections Registrar
Felicia Tan

IMMA *would like to thank*

Robin Marchesi
Flan Flanagan
Estate of Barry Flanagan
Tate, London
Dublin City Gallery The Hugh Lane
Southampton Art Gallery
S.M.A.K, Ghent
Joanna Melvin, Plubronze Ltd., London
Waddington Galleries, London

Contents

Foreword

IMMA started this collection of books a few years ago, with the intention of publishing interviews and writings with or by artists in its collection. So far we have published an interview with Michael Craig-Martin and two lectures given by Anne Madden and Louis le Brocquy respectively. From the start, however, we knew we had to be flexible with this format – as one always should be when dealing with art and artists – and we now find ourselves publishing a novella, or short novel, written by writer and poet Robin Marchesi (b. 1951, Hampshire, England). This text is a remembrance of the time he spent with artist Barry Flanagan in Ibiza, Barcelona, Amsterdam and London in the 1990s when Barry had asked him to put his archive of drawings into some kind of order. In his writing, Robin manages to convey with incredible precision the way Barry spoke, especially when he wanted to be serious. Barry Flanagan spoke in a way that could be described as pataphysical. Pataphysics is the name of a "science" conceived by French author Alfred Jarry (1873–1907), a precursor of surrealism. One of his most famous works, besides the play *Ubu Roi*, is the novel *Les gestes et opinions du docteur Faustroll, pataphysicien* (written in 1889, but only published in 1911), where Jarry describes pataphysics as "the Science of Imaginary Solutions". All through this book Jarry uses absurd humour to make fun of scientific language and traditional literature. Indeed, all his work can be seen as a hilarious attack on all sorts of bourgeois conventions. Jarry was to influence many artists from Joan Miró to Boyd Webb and Panamarenko, as well as writers such as Raymond Roussel, Julio Cortázar, Walter Abish and Georges Perec. Barry Flanagan, a great fan of Jarry himself, named his son Alfred after him.

Marchesi's adventures with Barry could somehow be described as the jests and opinions of Flanagan. I saw Barry a lot in the 1990s while I lived in Barcelona, and certainly remember quite a few conversations with him of the nature of those to be found in Robin's text. At the time, I also met many of the characters in the book – Barry's mother Monica, Renata, Jeny and Anu – even I am mentioned in the narrative. I had met Barry in 1992 when I began preparing a retrospective exhibition of his work in the Fundació "la Caixa" in Madrid, which toured to the Musée des Beaux-Artes in Nantes (1993–1994). We became good friends. In Spain he also befriended Majorcan artists Susy Gómez and Miquel Barceló, made prints with Joan Roma in Barcelona and ceramics with Joanet Artigas in Gallifa, a small city nearby. He also had shows in Tecla Sala and the Toni Tàpies Gallery in Barcelona. Somehow, Barry had a reputation of being kind of retired at this time, but he did a lot of work. Robin Marchesi, a close friend of Barry, was very fond of Ibiza where he spent a considerable amount of time, He also spent time in Venice Beach (California), Goa (India) and Bali (Indonesia), favourite spots by many people of what would be described the 1960s generation. Robin has published several books of poetry, including *A.B.C. Quest* (1991), *Kyoto Garden* (1996), *My Heart Is As* (2003) and also his early memoirs *A Small Journal of Heroin Addiction* (2000), and, like Barry, was an admirer of the Beat writers like Ginsberg, Burroughs and Kerouac as well as the Scottish author Alexander Trocchi, whom both of them knew. His writing, like the writings of the afore mentioned, is autobiographical, passionate, unconventional, fast, emotional and poetic. This book we now publish is a celebration of life, art and friendship.

Ibiza has attracted many creative people since the beginning of the twentieth century – philosophers such as Walter Benjamin and Emil M. Cioran; architects Josep Lluis Sert and Ron Arad; filmmakers Roman Polanski, Orson Welles and Barbet Schroeder; writers Pierre Drieu la Rochelle, Albert Camus, Jacques Prévert, Tristan Tzara, Rafael Alberti, Cees Nooteboom, Hugo Claus, Janet Frame, Norman Lewis and Martin Suter; artists Raoul Haussman, Zush or Erwin Bechtold; and musicians from bands like King Crimson, Pink Floyd, Can or Queen, as well as, later on, all the major DJs. Before he died, Barry, who was very happy in Ibiza, considered opening a Foundation near Santa Eulalia to house his collection and even engaged architects Pascal Cheikh-Djavadi and Victor Esposito to work on it, but eventually he changed his mind. It was a great pity.

Barry Flanagan also spent a lot of time in Ireland. He had a major show at IMMA in the summer of 2006, which I curated, and organised in collaboration with Dublin City Gallery The Hugh Lane, who presented some of his very large bronzes in O'Connell Street. Before that, in 1995, he had also shown in the Royal Hibernian Academy and an essay I had previously written for the Waddington Galleries in London was reproduced in the catalogue for that exhibition. That was my first text published in Ireland. Barry Flanagan also donated a major work, *The Drummer* (1996), to IMMA in 2001. The work is permanently installed at the entrance of our main building. IMMA later acquired *Carving No 6a* (1982) and a group of small ceramics, which were donated by Hester van Roijen. This book is being published just before a major exhibition of his work at the Tate later on this year.

We wish to thank Robin Marchesi for such a special text; the Estate of the artist; Leslie Waddington and the Waddington Galleries in London; and Barry's daughter Flan Flanagan for giving us permission to reproduce her portrait of Robin. At IMMA, I thank Christina Kennedy, Senior Curator and Head of the Collection, who manages this series of books, and her staff, especially Johanne Mullan, National Programmer who compiled and co-edited this book in the series.

Enrique Juncosa, Director

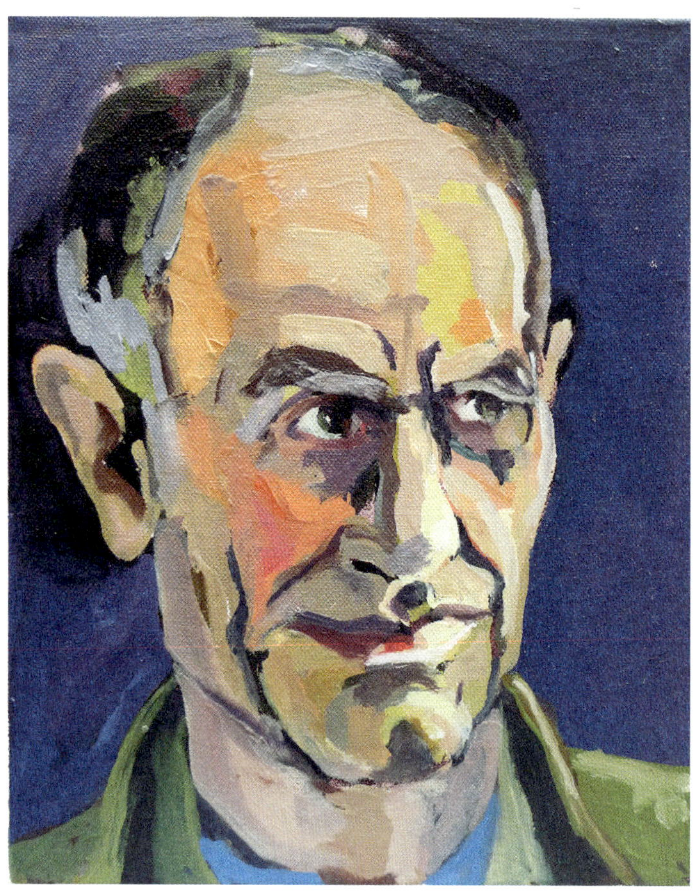

Flan Flanagan
'Poet Marchesi' (Robin), 2010
Oil on canvas - 30 x 25 cm

Poet of the Building Site

Robin Marchesi

"But I had then to organise this – a little 'jeu de sprit', it's been called – this is to take a book out of the library and Barry Flanagan was a student there, and Barry was the one student who did understand what I was talking about.

And he would meet me in the pub at lunch time and we would talk over a beer at lunch, and wouldn't see each other because I was employed in the painting department and he was a budding student in the sculpture department, and it wasn't the thing for the two departments to have anything to say to each other.

And I was trying to say look, the dimensional framework is simply misunderstood. The idea of three dimensions of space is inert and it is purely for the business of measuring up the house, and the bits and pieces of the house and for going down the street, and getting round the world. Otherwise it is not what's going on. It doesn't show us what is going on. And that was the meat of what I wanted to put into the School. But it also again happened when I invited – Barry and I invited – a number of these members of the College to my place to party, and the party was called 'Still and Chew'. I knew what was going to happen. And they were presented with a book out of the library by Clement Greenberg and it was called *Art and Culture*, and I had picked it as one of the relevant titles to have them chew up."

John Latham in conversation with Jacob Jakobsen, 2006.

From: "Interview with John Latham about the London Anti-University, his relation to knowledge, and what it means to chew a book." *Flat Time HO*, Peckham, June 2, 2003.
By Jakob Jakobsen. © Jakob Jakobsen 2006.

Barry Flanagan was a monumental sculptor whose contribution to twentieth- and twenty-first-century art is without parallel.

He walked a fine tightrope between madness and genius, and he knew it. One morning in the early 1990s he called me. I had not heard from him for six months:

"Hello Robin," he said as I answered the phone and as if we had conversed yesterday.

He spoke in a soft, almost apologetic tone.

"I didn't wake you?"

"No Barry."

"Have you time to come to the 'Groucho' and accompany me to the Foundry?"

"Certainly Barry."

I arrived in Dean Street and went up to his room.

He opened the door with a swooping gesture and ushered me in.

His appearance was in complete contrast to his voice on the phone.

He wore a barely closed, loosely tied, blue kimono; his eyes were large, staring and bulbous. His grey locks were tussled and dishevelled, almost as if his hair stood on end. His unshaven features suggested a night of debauchery.

His hands seemed huge, reddish, swollen and the atmosphere in the space of the room electrifying. He pulled back his lips in a silent welcome. I felt as if I had stepped into Wonderland. Again he motioned and my eyes followed his movement.

Amongst an apparent chaos of material stood a perfectly formed Hare. He had created it overnight, in red dental wax, over a thin metal armature.

It was this creation with which he had wrestled all night rather than my wilder assumptions.

The Hare wore a top hat and had one paw outstretched forward in a polite gesture of welcome.

It was an awesome sight.

He opened the door again.

"Have a coffee in the bar, I will join you there," he ordered, bending low, almost mimicking the poses of his sculpture.

He repeated the same swooping bow with which he had greeted me as he ushered me out of the room.

On the silent journey that morning to the East End of London, Barry offered one solitary observation:

"It's a hung jury on whether I am mad or not."

There is intensity about genius, which is not easy to define, or to bear. It can be both cruel and kind. Either way it originates from a concentrated sensitivity of emotion translated into form, by the mind.

∽ 2 ∽

A year or so earlier I had received a similar call from Flanagan, having just returned from my mother's funeral in Minorca.

After not seeing me for a year Barry invited me to accompany him to Fairfield Halls in Croydon to the 'Young Composer of the Year' performance.

It was a long drive and we made polite conversation about our respective families, before witnessing a wonderful piece performed on cello, an instrument Barry held close to his heart.

On the return journey we hardly spoke, although at one point Barry broke the silence with an obscure, yet direct comment:

"My brother is my engineer in the sky."

The words reverberated like a mantra.

It was an observation made almost as matter of fact yet was so exact in reaching the heart of the matter in relation to my own emotions regarding my recently deceased mother.

He meant it that way, for he was referring to his favourite brother Michael, who was lost at sea in the Observer 'Round the World Yacht Race'.

His linocut entitled *Atlantic Moon*, which the Tate has so beautifully reproduced, contains a hint of his brother's passing. The naïve, simple 'nightscape' contains the innocence of Saint-Exupéry's *Le Petit Prince*.

The extraordinarily haunting azul blue of this linocut has an intensely solitary solidarity. It is the boat of a ghost, crossing the river of Styx, to the other world. The work was conceived during a period when his drawing and printmaking were prolific.

I was struck how he used the present tense to describe his dead and closest brother. The statement had a revelatory quality that echoed into my own mourning. It was an act of great compassion and sensitivity toward me he displayed that day.

This was often the case in Barry's life. He had the talent to turn base metal to gold through an apparently off-hand remark.

More often than not these transmutations were lost, never received, the gold in them ignored.

As Rilke said of Rodin:

"He was a worker whose only desire was to penetrate with all his forces into the humble and difficult significance of his tools. Therein lay a certain renunciation of Life, but in just this renunciation lay his triumph, for Life entered into his work."[1]

☙ 3 ❧

"Hello," again the soft temperate voice.

It was August 1997 and I had been working intensely with Barry for almost a year.

"How are things?"

I gave him a rough approximation of how things stood regarding the 'project' we were involved with.

"Could you come over here?"

"To Ibiza?" I stuttered, incredulously.

"There are drawings that I would like you to find."

His voice, though retaining its seductive timbre, included an added edge.

"Certainly Barry, when would you like me to come?"

"Well . . . No need to waste time," he commanded and put the phone down.

He knew I would be there speedily.

---

1. Rainer Maria Rilke, *Auguste Rodin*, 1903.

Before I take the reader on this particular magic carpet ride I must briefly explain how this project came into being.

In the summer of 1996, a young artist called Chris Landoni and I gave a performance we entitled *Suicide by Hallucination*.

It was based on a chapter in a book entitled *The Banquet Years* by a man called Roger Shattuck.

Chris was young, badly educated, intelligent and pushy. He was much younger than I was. It was his enthusiasm that drove me to create the play.

I had, with trepidation, invited Barry to the Gate Theatre in London. I did not expect him to appear but Chris was very hopeful of meeting him and I was surprised, as the lights dimmed, to catch Barry sitting almost anonymously in the audience.

It added to the 'first and last' night nerves coursing through me, as we took to the stage.

The performance was a great success. Barry seemed to orchestrate an unplanned after party, which further flushed our temporary stardom.

Toward the end of this 'pataphysical' celebration, Barry drew Chris and I aside.

"Would you two like to help me with a project?" he enquired seriously.

"Certainly Barry," I replied for us both.

"I would pay of course," he added with his customary measure.

"Say, £100 a day, each?" he concluded.

I looked at Chris whose eyes replied silently.

"Thank you Barry," I said trying not to show emotion.

"Okay, the studio. Tomorrow, ten in the morning, on parade!"

He got up swiftly, paid the bill and, almost unnoticed, was gone.

Suffice to say that about 10 hours later, Chris and I were at AB Foundry in the London East End.

Barry met us and took us to his large, New-York-loft size studio, situated in Poplar, very close to the Blackwall Tunnel. The building that was arranged over two floors had been transformed and rebuilt in the 1970s by the artists who occupied them.

Flanagan had explained his project and how he wanted us to help him complete it. It included moving everything on the two floors to Barcelona.

He had sent Chris to look at the studio above and he brought out his chequebook:

"You do still have a bank account Robin?" he asked as he began writing.

"£2000 should get you started," he decided, compassionately.

"Thank you very much Barry," I replied sincerely and politely.

He tore out the cheque, handed it to me and I put it away discreetly.

"Well," he said gently, "I guess we better get started."

There was a quizzical air to the remark. He slightly raised an eyebrow in anticipation as if he was inquisitive to know where I would begin.

After the boost to my flagging bank balance I was enthusiastic.

My eyes perused the vast array of apparently, 'higgledy-piggledy' gatherings that the space seemed to contain.

After a long, awkward silence I stood up and announced, determinedly: "I better get started."

Next to my chair and in the path of all passing, or anyone walking through the studio, was a small crumbled Baluchi carpet.

I bent down and began rolling it up.

Suddenly Barry jumped out of his seat. His face was contorted in anger and his tone completely changed had become threatening, angry.

No longer a soft, gentle Hare one would wish to fawn, but a real male, boxing for its status:

He was rigid, fists clenched and shouting:

"Leave it alone! It's a fucking sculpture!"

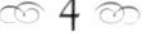

4

I arranged my itinerary speedily and the following afternoon was on the flight to Ibiza.

I had certain apprehensions for I knew the island well.

One of the many legends regarding Ibiza is that it is a 'Scorpio Isle'. The metaphor of seduction followed by a lethal dose was a common allegory there. I knew this from personal experience, the sting in its tail.

My previous exit from the island in 1992, as Barry witnessed, was ignominious to say the least.

Hence I travelled with a sense of trepidation, imagining many a disastrous or surprising permutation of possibilities that awaited me on my return to the Magic Isle.

Barry met me at the airport and we drove to Dalt Vila, high up in the old town. We dined tastefully above the bay overlooking the port before driving east down the coast through Santa Eulalia to his house. I guess with each kilometre I felt more at home.

Indeed, by the time we arrived at Flanagan's house I wondered what had possessed me to think of a 'sting in the tail'.

The following morning I awoke as Barry knocked on the door.

He wore his green suit and dark glasses.

"Morning Robin. There's coffee downstairs. Monica died in the night."

"I'm very sorry to hear that Barry," I said, very much awake and jumping out of bed.

I went downstairs to the kitchen. Anu, a Danish woman, who cared for Barry's mother Monica, was in tears. She was also the housekeeper and secretary of Barry's life in Ibiza.

"You know when to turn up, don't you?" she said to me. We had known each other many years.

I sipped my coffee as they wheeled the stretcher containing Monica's body across the pebbled pathway.

∽ 5 ∾

During the following days I saw little of Barry. He was preoccupied with his mother's passing. Nevertheless I already had my 'brief' and set about my task of gathering together his sketches.

Flanagan had been predictably vague as to their whereabouts. The extremely imprecise nature of their location was amplified by the blank stares of those in the house whom I questioned on the drawings' existence.

For three days I sought them everywhere and managed from some obscure places to assemble nearly a hundred.

Barry had a precise way he wished these creations to be digitally filed.

As a result, one became quite intimate with each piece. His skill with line was unparalleled and mesmerising.

Under a bed I found a Daler notebook whose angular penned drawings, once studied, took on vast dimensions and proportions. Cosmic notation, octaves of a giant scale, the music of spheres, was suggested by the delicate yet forceful hand that created these exquisite works.

One series he did with his left hand clearly illustrated how we utilise different parts of the brain. As I contemplated them with the poetic sensitivity Barry respected, I was interrupted by Anu.

"Barry's back Robin. He'd like you to come to the kitchen for a meal," she said.

"Right I'll be five minutes." I was surprised.

Barry's kitchen faced west with a view of pine trees and fields. At one end was all the kitchen paraphernalia, at the other a long table and an Augur fire.

The room was empty when I arrived save for two cheese sandwiches, two glasses and a full bottle of scotch.

Also on the table was a firebrick.

I already knew not to touch anything.

There was a dimly lit side lamp and candles throwing off a shadowy glow as the sky began twinkling mysteriously with Balearic stars.

The past few days had electrified me with their intensity and I was apprehensive about how Barry would be. We had not spoken since his mother Monica had passed on.

I was just beginning to wonder where Barry was when he appeared as if from nowhere.

He walked over to the table, opened the whiskey, poured two large glasses and offered me one, pulling back his lips at the same time.

It was a gesture that suggested you did not refuse the offer.

I took my glass and we chinked them together before drinking deeply. Barry was dressed in a particular Japanese kimono from his collection. It was blue and embroidered with white dragons that matched the colour of his long, tussled locks.

He wore only a pair of short white socks on his feet.

Under the kimono he had a *Leaping Hare* T-shirt and pants.

His face was unshaven and his eyes hidden behind dark, thick, Gucci sunglasses.

He took one of the sandwiches and began munching, as if grazing, while his other hand moulded invisible clay between thumb and forefinger. He made a gesture indicating I also ate and once more I accepted his invitation.

He continued his hand movement, sniffing the air for scent, as he stared at the distant stars twinkling more and more, as twilight descended.

He sighed, put the sandwich down, refilled our glasses and stared at the firebrick.

"Why, if I signed it like Carl Andre it would become a work of art!" he exclaimed with a jocular lilt.

"I shall do it." He pulled a Mont Blanc fountain pen from his kimono pocket and signed the brick with a flourish.

"One firebrick signed!" he declared proudly and dramatically.

He had a way of emphasising words and whispering others.

To hear what Flanagan said demanded a degree of concentration, which excluded time contemplating one's self.

It meant being silent inside, to not have opinion or question, but to just absorb. Otherwise the 'whole' was lost and it became nonsense.

"Have you got your notebook?"

There was a hint in his tone that made me glad I did.

"Yes Barry."

"Good." He sat down.

 I followed suit, taking out my pen and book.

"The drawing is always the negative, Robin," he said breathing deeply. His voice was soft.

"Jarry was my first love with Paris," he revealed as he twirled his glass.

"John Latham," he continued, "reduced everything to a dot!" He smiled at the recollection before whimsically continuing:

"The laughter in art as in *Silens* at St Martin's College of Art, 1964–1965."[2] I wrote swiftly, silently, trying to be nothing more than a fly on the wall.

"Ha!" he exclaimed.

---

2. The students at St. Martins, on a Roladex published *Silens* and Barry was very much a driving force in its production.

"I wield a very straight bat. And sometimes my own balls," he lifted an eyebrow.

"Now there is a letter to write." He bent down mimicking a cricketing stroke.

I was bowled over by the statement but had no time to contemplate it. Barry continued:

"My artistic career began at the Royal Bristol College of Art where I used to be a model in life drawing. 1957," he announced, becoming more erect, holding his head up proudly at the achievement.

He was out of his chair and pacing the room like he was on stage.

He turned to me and pointed with his glass:

"If there is any portrait in this book it comes from you in public.

What you and I know, as the individual, in the face of mass murder. These works are not intended to aggravate the schism." He paused, his last statement a plea almost.

He walked over to the table and poured himself another, slightly diluted, drink.

"More water," he remarked as he noted the glass.

"Desalination . . . more geometry and that is abstract. Less dots!" he concluded, returning to his original comments.

"You need a victim for bad jokes," he paused as if looking into a misty realm.

"An erroneous context, portraiture," he observed.

"Just as a reference, the construct of real time, as a bronze sculpture, is cerebral to my practice as a sculptor."

"I've been doing it about 35 years now and I'll never do it alone again,"
he decided.

"1962–63 used to write letters and pin them on boards," he drank deeply. "Bit of a graffiti artist," he amusingly reminisced, mimicking Keith Haring.

"And the letter to Tony Caro was quite fundamental. I would like the privée[3] to read it again!" His tone was demanding, angry, challenging.

"At this stage in my life am I looking for a publisher, or craving interesting reading?" He said this incredulously.

---

3. "Privée" has a double meaning here. It means 'privacy', but it is also an old slang, for "privet" or "toilet".
The letter he refers to was one he published in *Silens* magazine (1962) in which he challenges Caro's view of what sculpture is.

"My input," he qualified, "such as it is, required the concentration of an engineer, the poetic form and the will to communicate." It was a bold and forceful statement with a ring of truth that resonated through the atmosphere of the room.

"The civility of *Potlatch*."[4] He referred obliquely to the 'Situationists' and the obscure magazine of the 'Imaginist Bauhaus' movement.

"Whoops!" he exclaimed as he paced the floor and put his hand over his mouth.

"Is these days as volatile as derision and vulgar ness," he concluded.

A slight pause before in a much gentler tone he began again:

"Laughter as the Pataphysicans might have it and the struggle with humour that torments the Doctor, Jonathan Miller." He fawned the name. His tone had become sarcastic and then he added, "Is no idle speculation to imagine debate."

He held his hands together in prayer bowing three times for each word:

"Granta . . . Granta . . . Granta." He sneered the publisher's name sanctimoniously.

"¿Far too volatile to take place in public? And write that down Spanish style with a question mark at the beginning and end," he ordered and then, once more, in his softer tone:

"Thirty five years in this school and have within it sustained that presence, such as it is." There was a slight pause as he took a deep intake of breath.

"And my retirement from trade should be viewed as a result of the phrasing of this schooling. References to the social contract are not barred." A satisfactory nod of the head accompanied this observation.

"And hopefully the portrait will not be illegible."

He finished on a definite note and paused in his pacing. He turned toward the window. His left arm was bent behind his back.

In his right, he swirled his glass as he spoke on. This time like a businessman to his secretary he began dictating a letter to an art critic:

"Dear David Sylvester,

To preside over a body of work is only physically an edge to the anaesthesiologist's contemplation.

---

4. *Potlatch* was a magazine produced by the 'Situationists'.

Not wishing to preside over any future museum showing this work, I'm looking for men in my boat."

There was a challenge in the invitation.

Suddenly his voice became faraway, soft, and almost inaudible, as if he spoke to another dimension.

"The kissing's so quick and the voyages slick, as a passage from here to there. Tell me what happened?"

This poetic, gentle, moment was brief:

"Okay . . . Round One!"

"I hope I'm not unearthing any old chestnuts, much better new potatoes, to give form to the passage of the past.

"And physically I shall clean up that imagery," he paused, sipped and muttered the word, "pataphysical", before returning to his previous flow.

"Though the objectification of thought remains a cumbersome one, given its physicality."

Again the whimsical pause came into play. There was something awkward and yet precise in his movement. His performance of this unplanned script was Brechtian, Beckett like.

Yet, despite the background of his recently deceased mother, like all his creations it had, at root, Jarry's Theatre of the Absurd.

"Self consciously I took up sculpture as a challenge," he stated proudly. "This sentiment goes back 35 years and while I've never completed anything on my own . . . fascination be wild in this pack." He raised his leg so his pose was like his *Nijinski Hare* as he spoke the final phrase.

Then he relaxed back into his own musings:

"The contra-distinction between laughter and humour is knowledge to me. Got any stones that need breaking?" His face lit up mischievously, his eyes wandered around the room falling on various stone objects.

"That little bit of Zen, a better part of me." There was a great sadness conveyed in this statement which he laughed off:

"That was very sudden . . . ignore me . . . ignore me."

Though he could not completely throw off this sensitive vibration, for as he walked over to a small stone sculpture, he said:

"I used to do it without being asked," he used hand gestures to emphasis his point:

"Appraise it . . . think about it . . . appropriate it . . . is there any simple geometry in it?

"A construct between the dot and its companions in (. . .) communication?" He concluded with a reference once more to John Latham and then turned to me.

I could tell that behind his Gucci glasses he was studying me intently. Only my fingers on the pen had moved, as Barry had verbalised this soliloquy:

"A professional couldn't get this out of me," he said gently, "volunteered such as it is."

"The sorrows of nat . . . u . . . ral loss," he emphasised each syllable clearly, "are a seed of anger in me. The portrait of the physical world is a treasure to me when speaking of the image."

He seemed far away as he poured himself another whiskey; so solitary he was surprised I was there.

"I began to reflect as if I was writing on my own," he said raising his eyebrows with shock, "and forgot . . . I had something to say!"

He turned to me:

"Thank you Doctor," he said this directly like I was a psychiatrist. He turned to a picture of Rowan Atkinson on a magazine cover: "Mr Bean," he acknowledged and finally, raising his eyes to the heaven:

"Monsieur Jarry as your student, I say, hurrah!" He drank deeply our health and I silently joined him in the toast.

He grinned and delicately moved forward, took my now empty glass, refilled and returned it. He had a way sometimes where his movement was close to an invisible dance. I thought he had finished but he hadn't. There was more to come:

"We have imagination por favor," he exclaimed strongly and then corrected himself. "One," he emphasised the word, "has imagination por favor."

"Imagination is really fundamental as regards my upbringing. Emblematically speaking, Mr Jarry is a great pal in this schoolyard and next to him I would celebrate the powers of interpretation along with invention." He sat down and drummed his fingers on the table while contemplating momentarily his signed firebrick.

"Tiddly pom-pom-pom."

He paralleled the naïve clarity of Jarry's imagined solution with an unspoiled innocence that resonated in his words.

"I wasn't on the beaches playing with the girls. I only played with Dinky cars," he remembered casually, but warmly.

The impression he conveyed of the lonely child on a Welsh beach was overpowering, almost visual in the strange half-light of that Ibicenco early morning.

"My alliance with Jarry has indeed been a professional one. Never ever being a good student but I felt something," he recognised.

His brown eyes shone as he reminisced on his youthful, unsullied, late teens.

"And I'm so happy to report that Nick and Corinne are grey, my neighbours that year."[5]

With a wistful sigh he continued:

"Pass me the *Evergreen* special on Pataphysics," he remembered.

He reached out as if accepting a copy.

"There's a sack of coal, a pint of ale and a good wish or two in it, rurally speaking." He recreated a long forgotten era, brought it into the present. It conjured up images of a hopeful youth:

"That 'gargantuan splendiferousness,'" he skipped two decades.

"That zender industrial ness!" he thundered, puffing out his chest proudly.

"As author I personally celebrate all the work generously completed @ 'Factor-If-Foundry.'"

He became larger than life like he was 'Pere Ubu' 'hornstrumpetting' on Fawe Street.

"Write like you are on a computer," he suddenly commanded and walked over to verify my scrawling of the @ symbol and not actually written 'at'.

Satisfied I was writing *ad verbatim* he relaxed and continued:

"Some of this predisposition to invent linguistically has in my memory been taken seriously; while eradication and exactitude have not been challenged." He seemed incredulous.

"I just want to conform to some sense, as among civilians, a nod is as good as a wink!"

He lifted one leg, touched his forehead with his glass and smiled.

Suddenly, he removed his sunglasses and looked at me directly.

---

5. Nick and Corrine Wadley. Nick lived next door to Barry when he was first in London and introduced Barry to Jarry.

His eyes were red and swollen with grief: "I'm not going up a mountain with a bag of rice and far be it from this frame to haunt you, to even wish to haunt you."

He put his glasses back on and looked out of the window:

"Others live along with all these observations, is nothing the individual can't handle. So on your John Wayne's white motorcycle!"

For the final time he drained his glass.

Outside night had begun to slowly lighten and the outline of the large pine trees swaying in the wind began to take shape. Not far away, sunrise was on the distant horizon.

"You'll be ready for the boat from Denia tomorrow?" Flanagan enquired as if the previous hours had not existed.

"Yes, Barry," I lied, shocked by the immediacy of his plans.

It was about five on Saturday morning.

"Good, now, give me your book," he demanded.

He signed one of the pages:

"Just in case there is any dispute later," he explained and handed it back to me.

"Well, thank you and good night." He smiled.

"Fine Barry," I smiled back, shook his proffered hand and took it as my cue to exit right.

6

By mid morning, about thirty hours later, Flanagan and I entered the artfully packed Ford Scorpio. I had spent the intervening time gathering together what needed to be taken on our travels.

I had barely managed to sleep, for taking in the perceptions of what Flanagan had said was hardly conducive to a good nights rest.

He had reappeared Sunday lunchtime, and looked like he had also not slept.

Flanagan and I, each in our individual ways, bleary eyed and eccentric, tried to look as normal as possible as we entered the smart car and drove, in silence, from the east to the west of the island, each locked in our own individual thoughts.

We arrived in the port of San Antonio, bought our tickets, parked the car on the boat and went to the deck. It was extraordinarily hot, but Barry found a concrete pillar and sat down. He then promptly proceeded to fall asleep. We were among the first passengers on the ferry.

By the time of departure the boat had become fetid and humid. It was filled by up-all-night youngsters or tourists. Many of them I am sure had probably no wish, in the slightest, to ever leave Ibiza. I noticed how some stared vacantly, almost melancholically at the distance Isle of Vedra as it disappeared over the horizon.

Flanagan slept on, apparently blissfully unaware that we had even left port.

For the journey he wore his customary green tweed suit, shirt, tie and green peaked cap. Sweat poured from his brow, streaming down his face, and the front of his cotton shirt dripped.

"Is he alright?" concerned passengers asked me, or their companions, as they passed.

On several occasions I had to stop these citizens from shaking him by silently demonstrating, with a nod and a wink, that I was looking out for him.

Three hours later, as the mainland in the shape of Denia came into focus, Flanagan magically awoke. He wiped his moustache as if they were whiskers and got to his feet refreshed. He was ready to disembark for the long trip of 350 kilometres to Barcelona and was happier once we had berthed and were in the car. He liked to be moving.

We arrived at his Grand Via apartment and went inside. It was airless but he did not open the windows. He looked round it and returned.

"Very nice," he remarked and stood for a moment pondering before continuing:

"I think we'll keep travelling north," he suggested suddenly.

"Yes Barry," I replied getting out of my seat.

"Hasta luego Rioja and Bonjour Beaujolais," I merrily remarked as we left.

In a leap we were gone.

Several hours later on the French autoroute, near Lyon, we stopped for coffee.

The television showed an anarchic commotion in a Parisian tunnel I had travelled through not long ago.

Barry's face barely altered:

"Not all our Princesses should be sacrificed to erroneous behaviour," he muttered disdainfully.

Disgusted by the whole affair he got up and we carried on. Ten hours later we arrived in the Herengracht, Amsterdam.

It was midnight and the house was empty. We sat in silence at the kitchen table.

Simultaneously the bell tolled in the Westermart church.

"Its ringing will resonate to the heavens long after the laughter of these perceptions have ceased their song," I thought as it reverberated round the centre of the city.

Often, as I did then with Barry, one sensed a tension almost as if one's presence itself was a disturbance to him.

He lived in a unique world, with unique perceptions and even a cough at the wrong moment could bring about a look of black thunder.

I noted the whiskey bottle on the table and, as quietly as possible, got up, fetched two glasses and placed them on the table before sitting down again.

Barry made no comment which in itself was a bonus as a gesture such as I had just made might well have led to what I jokingly called, being "head butted by a goat."

This was an obtuse reference to Barry's astrological sign of Capricorn.

In the silence of sitting with Flanagan, obscure thoughts would enter one's mind, usually inevitably connected to something Flanagan had awoken in one's senses.

"This is not a dot," I thought, "nor a quest-ion, in the mark of time."

Flanagan reached forward and took the whiskey bottle, gently unscrewed it and filled our glasses in equal measure.

Then, he returned it to its original position, pursed his lips and began drumming his fingers on the table.

He pulled out his bulky mobile phone, opened it, put on his glasses and dialled a number. There was no reply and he closed it decisively and put it on the table in front of him, accompanied by the spectacles.

"Jeny isn't in," he stated.

"Mind you," he added. "It's the beginning of the month and the rent has to be paid."

He smiled, reassured she would make contact soon.

Indeed, comforted by the thought, he raised his glass and drank before delicately placing it back on the table.

Tosilentlyobservethiswholeprocesswaslikewatchinglivingsculpture. Every movement Barry made had a sense of moulding life three dimensionally. It was an exquisite portrayal of the potential of being human and a privilege to witness. It reminded me of something Barry had once said as a throwaway remark but really, on another level, a very serious one:

"Sculpture should be performed like going for a swim."

He again lifted his glass and drank.

"Tomorrow," he instructed, "I want you to write to Enrique Juncosa on *Why the Hare?*"

"Yes Barry," I replied, totally uncertain of where to begin and he knew it.

"I'm off for some sleep." He got up and left me alone.

∽ 7 ∽

"Dear Enrique" I began the next morning.

I was reading, this morning, an essay by Barry entitled:

Why the Hare?

In it he adroitly attempts to explain how a moment of conceptual cognisance, regarding his impression of a Hare leaping over the Sussex Downs, was the catalyst for the form now manifest in his bronze sculptures.

This occurrence in 1970 took ten years of osmosis before it saw the light of day. He further explained how two other incidences affected this development.

Firstly, in 1974, while sketching in Tuscany he noted a figure in an otherwise uninhabited landscape who grew into a giant as he focused on his perspective. It was a shock of proportion in scale that was amplified two years later during a conference he attended at Loch Ness in Scotland.

Here Barry, while drawing, saw a duck on the Loch he first associated from a distance as the mythical Monster. He was, as he has told me, influenced by the content of the soirée the previous evening. He realised that by perspective what he saw as a part of a giant, was actually complete in itself.

A duck? When is a duck, not a duck? I recalled Barry's question as I paused before continuing writing:

After some considerable time now in Barry's presence the theme of the manifestation of an idea seems to have been ever prevalent in his work. The ability to reduce and expand, inhale and exhale exists in every sculptural composition materialised from his concepts.

This artistic integrity exists in all his work from the production of *Silens* magazine at St Martin's College of Art to the now famous Leaping Hares.

Evidence of this process can be clearly deciphered in his conceptual work of the 1960s when he openly challenged the traditional modes of sculptural form.

His installations were revolutionary in their day and justifiably caused fervour more sensational (than *Sensation* at the Royal Academy), when shown at the Tate Gallery.

These compositions were valued for their precision of idea.

This summer Barry and I attended the third year show at Chelsea Art College.

As we walked around the exhibits there was not one sculpture that did not have its root in the long forgotten address, adopted by Barry Flanagan and his pals, to the artistic establishment 30 years ago.

Interestingly enough, in the early 70s when the idea of conceptual sculpture became accepted, Barry stopped working in this form. He returned to more traditional roots and began drawing, making etchings and linocuts, working with stone, learning a trade, allowing that seed planted on the Sussex downs by a very brave hare to germinate and take root.

Barry applied the same figuration he employed in the 1960s with Hessian, rope, and sand to materialise a sculpture in bronze.

The original concept must be strong enough to allow the participation of others.

Even the geometric framework of his delegation has a sculptural angle. None of these large, delicately balanced monumental Hares would have come into being without the craftsmanship of the foundry or the acumen of the gallery.

The existence of an established order is vital for one of his concepts to take form.

The sculpture needs a firm base on which to lay its case and it is all hands to the deck regarding the whole process from the invisible thought made visible then manifested, be it a Pile or a Hare, the process of transmutation can only occur with the labour of those who command, as Barry puts it, 'civil respect'.

"Merde!" I wrote.

The shadow of Jarry can be seen in every aspect of Barry's work throughout his life and is not without significance, either professionally or personally. He began making Hares . . .

I stopped as the door burst open and suddenly Barry entered the room, interrupting my epistle on this subject.

He was dressed in one of his famous green suits, and his face was thunderous.

"Have you your book?" he demanded.

"Yes Barry."

"Good," he replied and sat down.

Let me add here that every time I visited that house on the Herengracht it was chaotic. Even a day later, this time it had been no different. My letter had been written against the background of the returning Jeny and her family, coupled with the arrival of Anu.

Barry's agenda, unfathomable as it was, gave a strangely odd order to a 'fluxus' as he called it whimsically. It was an obtuse reference to his early works with Yoko Ono.

Barry got up and began pacing the room, hands behind his back. His long white hair and beard gave him an almost Gandalf-like air, as he began dictating to me:

"Letter to *The Times*," he spoke officially and then, like one of his Hare's winking:

"Dear Sir,

Let not all our Princesses be sacrificed to erroneous behaviour!"

It came out like a plea but a hopeless one and then, without a breath almost, he reminisced to another age:

"Poetically speaking, correspondence, letters to *The Times*, are kind of traditional," he chuckled jazzily before becoming harder, reminiscing on another era.

"How Gaudia Brzeska felt throwing his carved sculpture, piece of work, through his gallery window in Cork Street."

He recollected the famous 1920s incident with a movement that illustrated the sculptor heaving and throwing his creation.

Then he suddenly stopped any movement:

"His acquaintance," he spoke as if to a ghost, before returning to the subject.

"Sculptors' hands have precedence in letters to *The Times*," he mused.

"At this threshold I'm a serious artist," he stated with an air of trying to convince himself. There was something definitely Jarryesque in his tone.

"Letters are an umbilical cord, the address is to the heavens, the imagination."

He looked upwards. There was a definitive note almost of despair in the sensitivity of this statement.

"St Peter's gate has been eroded by the West, too much cynicism." His voice trailed off, before resuming in a lighter vein:

"Don't be put off, I'm a serious artist," he reiterated.

"I remember when sculptors, post Second World War, including Henry Moore, switched to *The Guardian* and the club."

He raised his eyebrows before obliquely continuing:

"As a rugby player, I notice the evolution of my own build. You don't need determination, when you are fit." It came out like the long forgotten fact of life that it is.

He hardly paused before continuing:

"Dear Robin Marchesi,

"As I begin this story I'm so happy to remember the facility Leslie gave me," he referred to his gallery owner with great fondness.

"Number . . . what was it? In Clifford Street the basement of Choman's, Japanese for district. Where I won a Welsh, milky, angole settle, through my attention."

He thought aloud about that *Sixties Dish* sofa, struggling to make sense of how he came to terms with his continual inner attempts to distinguish between what he defined as 'Art' and 'Trade'.

"Letter to *The Times*," he again stated boldly.

"It's personal," he beseeched.

"The time which created the sculpture in that convent, not far from Cavendish Street."

He began pacing the room as if he was back in the 1960s learning, experimenting, honing his sculptural skills:

"My bruised knees, cartilage, square danced!" His eyebrows lifted.

"Fresh orange juice," he continued, though I was no longer certain he was in the past or present tense.

"Triangled out . . . references to the artist . . . my UB fort…tissimo . . ." He paused and looked at me.

"Write it down as I say!" he demanded before speaking slowly, even the dots in his dictation.

"For . . . ter . . . tis . . . im . . . oo . . ." He referred to a time when he was unemployed and unemployable.

Suddenly he returned to the present:

"Print it . . . R.O. Lienchovitz," he referred obscurely to Jeny's ex lover before suddenly doing a little dance:

"Robbie O Rembrandt . . . Cha-cha-cha," with which he concluded his jig.

"Busy hands for salvation," he sighed and sat down.

"I have no concept of this public life I'm subjected to . . . Oh civilians ahaa!"

He was on his feet again doing the little jig before, once more, appearing to be speaking to the dead, rather than the living:

"I'm kind of thinking of acquaintance . . . life remembered thus," again he emphasised and I follow his spelling:

"Zeitgeists . . . sts . . . sts . . . sts . . . acquainted muster . . . must . . .ter . . . ter . . . ter thus . . . with all acknowledgements." He paused and for a moment I hoped he had concluded, as following him was no easy task, let alone writing it down as well.

He added a postscript:

"Letter to The Editor:
    Drama to dust . . . knowledge must . . . does my beard grow long?"
    He contemplated the thought and stroked his face before finally concluding:
    "Thank you, I enjoyed that very much."
    With a grin in my direction he departed, as unexpectedly as he'd appeared.

Some months later Flanagan and I were again in the Herengracht.

The previous day we had spent our time transporting a grand piano out of the apartment. This was done by using a haulage system and required the removal of the large window overlooking the canal. It was a precise and skilled form of transportation and although the human element was minimal there was an aspect of mechanical dance, or performance, in the process. This was typical of Barry for, wherever he was in the world, he conducted a human symphony, orchestrated a ballet by interacting three-dimensional objects.

He brought life to the inanimate and, to an individual trying to understand the whole, it was chaotic.

One of Flanagan's struggles was with people who tried to comprehend what he was doing. In the many years I spent with him people would come and go.

At first they would prostrate themselves before him or fawn him, but quickly they would become too familiar and start telling him how his way of 'doing' could be improved on. Barry would often apparently acquiesce to them, say little, and be like a diffident leveret. This would encourage them to be bolder, more expansive and full of themselves. I had heard people like this ask for absurdities from Flanagan. He would astutely sidestep or deflect their requests.

Eventually and inevitably an evening would arise, when he would invite them to discuss their 'project'. Little did they know that after several hours in Barry's company perceptions would change and any attempt to keep up with him would result in a situation when the diffident leveret would transmute into a big brave, boxing, buck Hare, ready to jump into any fire. These people, as I said, came and went. They would disappear citing Flanagan as either unfathomable or foolish.

But he retained and needed a 'core' unit. Each with their own part, and wise enough to know that they did not know what he did.

It required precision, skill, sensitivity, like those performers that day in the Herengracht, simply moving a grand piano, while simultaneously sculpting for a sculptor.

Barry was very pleased at the extra space created by the absence of the grand piano.

Furthermore, that morning a parcel had arrived which, when I entered the room, he asked me to unwrap.

It contained a French magazine with a cover photo of Barry's *Leaping Hare*, installed on a hill, overlooking the vineyards of Haut Lafitte.

It was a stunning tribute to Flanagan's work and also showed great respect to traditional mythology, that the finest grapes would be grown in the sight of the Hare.

A letter accompanied the illustration thanking Barry for his creation and asking him to accept the enclosed gift.

Barry got out of his chair and came over. He studied the picture while stroking his beard. He looked quite odd in his long khaki shorts, kimono and sandals. He clasped his hands firmly behind his back.

He turned to me and grinned then looked down at the wooden box, inviting me to do the same:

"Haut Lafitte Premier Cru 1972" was carved into it.

"Hmmm," murmured Barry and raised his eyebrows mischievously.

He quickly found an appropriate tool and opened the box.

Six bottles beautifully packed in straw stood before us. Barry picked one up studied it, opened it, smelled it, poured two glasses and drank:

"Very nice," he remarked satisfied and indicated I try the nectar.

I accepted the invitation gratefully, perhaps knowing I might not drink such fine wine again.

The whirl of an incoming fax began as I sat down.

Barry could tell by sound when it was complete and went to study the message. He ripped it off the receiver harshly, indicating the communication had disturbed him.

He returned to his chair and threw the offending paper on the carpet and drank decisively. He picked up a book on the table beside him.

It was the life of Stravinsky by Robert Craft and I, under Flanagan's tutelage, was reading it. He flicked nonchalantly through the pages and sneered.[6]

"Take out your book and pen and take this down," he said suddenly and got up to refill our glasses.

He saw I was ready pen poised over my Smythson notebook.

He paced the floor and began:

------

6. Robert Craft, *Stravinsky: Glimpses of a life*, 1992.

"I turned my back on books to take up sculpture as a language and all I'm left with is Feng Shui. Now you tell me who's keeping their act together?" There was anger in his tone.

He bent down and picked up the fax:

"Cuckoos don't just lay eggs. They break other peoples'" he remarked as a matter of fact, before once more dismissing the paper.

His eyes fell on the Stravinsky book.

"The Rite of Spring," he repeated the name of Stravinsky's famous work with nostalgia, before switching modes.

"Perfect place to start. Why I began dancing at thirty-two. Sue introduced me to the Rite of Spring and Jean Cocteau. Mind you I was moving in the same circles. We were both students."

There was fondness in his eyes, as there always was, when he spoke of his former wife.

"I was introduced to her by Roland Muldoon, also of the Bristol Old Vic, at a performance of *The Soldier's Tale*."[7] He spoke of his old friend who re-invented, with Barry's assistance, The Hackney Empire in London.

"The Rite of Spring," he repeated it as a mantra, like he was resurrecting a long forgotten innocence.

"The zeitgeist, the spirit of the age, in a civilian sense," he paced up and down, further explaining this verbal concept.

"I mean spirit as that member which is not part of a congregation. Herded into seats."

He derisorily continued:

"Clockwork Orange; the graffiti of shock and that puts Hollywood in its place next to the creative form." In an instant he explained the unoriginality of film as a medium. Its affiliation to organised religion.

"The civil mind rules the life," hope filled his timbre.

"Yes!" he exclaimed and then looked down at the crumpled fax.

"Never mind going round with an egg in your hand shouting chicken.

---

7. Igor Stravinsky *The Soldier's Tale* 1918.

'Create the egg," he demanded.

"And don't speak to me of courage, rather than implication. Application.
Do it. Piss off."

I squirmed quietly on my seat for the fax had been from Chris Landoni. Indeed Flanagan had shown a great interest in his development. Chris's fax showed and explained his studies with Rosemarie Trockel in Germany. Nevertheless the sketches of 'cups' were directly from his exposure to Barry's skill with the pen. Hence the reference to cuckoos, for an artist must develop originality and make their own egg.[8]

"The Rite of Spring," he repeated, introducing his next observation: "The middle classes all turn up on time for the musician or the performer. And Joseph Beuys when he said, 'everyone was an artist', supplied no content."

He paused and pondered, "And that's up to the individual," a short silence before, " 'spirit', 'guts', 'no question'."

Each of these last three he spoke with a pause for digestion.

"Knowledge," he continued quickly, "is not a safety vault. Drivers know the expedient is the chain in our minds," he obliquely referred to the flexibility of the individual's choice.

"Zeitgeist," he repeated.

By this time the effect of the high quality Château Haut Lafitte had deepened my perceptions and I am sure Barry's too.

"As part-time astronauts," he observed with a twinkle in his eye as he looked at me.

"I know, you know. You know, you know. Meg." His ending referred to the woman in *Titanic*, the film we had watched two days ago.

While still attempting to take in his last statement, Barry had already dramatically changed the scenario:

"Now if I met Allen Ginsberg at the gates with St Peter. I'm not proud I'd pass." He continued with a sideways grin.

"Looks like Mr Burroughs is my surgeon." He stopped, contemplating the heavenly vision before him.

---

8. Chris Landoni (1972 – 2005) was an artist and student/assistant of Barry Flanagan.

"No thank you Doc." He decided. "Dark dude."

His eyes widen dramatically as he humorously completed the phantasmagoria:

"That could have been lifted off a wavy vinyl!" he stated dramatically.

The Invisible Insurrection, a treatise by Trocchi, had some of the spirit of Alfred Jarry," he spoke as if I was not there.[9]

"To a power Trocchi's modesty remains an empowerment," he continued and then froze for a moment in movement.

"No inheritance," the energy of his observation pervaded the room.

It seemed that the spirit of Alex Trocchi had been raised, from the video we watched of him yesterday, to a living incarnation.

The spectrum of the room deepened:

"This is not information it is expression!
This is not information it is expression!
This is not information it is expression!"

He spoke the phrase slowly emphasising it, watching me write it, three times.

As he spoke it seemed his voice altered an invisible octave as he verbalised the phrase from each part of himself.

That fine balanced harmony he possessed, through life experience, which enabled originality.

I had no time to pause.

"Renata was a student of Beuys," he reflected as he refilled our glasses, though the process was more a dance than an offering.[10]

"She remains an art student. That's middle class and fatty with responsibility for the blobs, without being dirty." Here he raised his glass, grinned, and opened his bulging eyes wider. It was deriding and endearing, simultaneously.

"They've arrived, demanding to be fed and that is not a fiscal exchange." He fin-

---

9. Alexander Trocchi, *A Revolutionary Proposal: Invisible Insurrection of a Million Minds,* 1963.
10. Renata is the mother of Alfred and Annabelle.

ished on a surprised, naïve note.

"The mind knows or repose!" He quoted the title of one of his works. In the ambiance of the occasion the double meaning was blatant.

"Tate Gallery is showing *A Nose in Repose*," he pursed his lips proudly and put on his OBE:

"See you in the Tate Gallery. School caps and all!" he joked, touching his forelock with his knuckle, before suddenly continuing, far more seriously:

"This is a press release and I expect to see it printed," he ordered darkly and in the same tone, he returned to his misty past:

"I didn't waste time demonstrating outside the Tate Gallery for free entry which is everyone's privilege!" There was something jocular in his political observations. It led him onto another subject entirely.

"Regards to your uncle Eric and your cousin, didn't she fuck me over? What a bright spark," he concluded.

He referred to a night some 35 years previously, when a relation of mine had left a deep impression on him.

"I've been thrown out of better garden parties than this, may I say?" he continued.

"And one thing about the video is one never knows when it stops with regard to conversation sensually being that ignition, bids me caution, to know when to conclude."

Finally he paused for me to take in the surreality of his language.

"When to stop," he mused on, "some composure."

"After all, music claims composition as composure." It was as if he was asking himself a question whose answer he sought in sculpture, a form that had only the laws of space for its fundamental structure.

It meant I had no more import in Barry's present sculptural moment than the crumpled fax from Chris Landoni.

But I had no time to be distracted for Flanagan continued regardless of any perception I might have of what words I wrote.

I knew this, that to contemplate what he had just said was like Orpheus looking over his shoulder for Eurydice. I would be lost to Hades.

"In the olden days there was some alternative to composition," he thought back not too far.

"As a sculptor to trail the desert with a stick," he said it whimsically, referring I think to a work by Richard Long, and then obscurely relating:

"Regards to that rock Mr Beckett." He lifted his glass and drank to a ghost.

"Waiting for the inevitable from outer space, maybe Dylan Thomas is the chain?" His brow furrowed then lightened as he joked:

"Brendan Behan as the past participle!"

"That teenage dumble, and snob yer nobbery," he flexed his elbows as he spoke.

"Ground out that space boy, oy oy oy oy!" he ordered as he got up and danced momentarily.

"Wave. Agree." He waved at the invisible as he walked to the table and opened another bottle before continuing, very slowly:

"The sustention of attention sounds like survival to me."

He pulled the cork and continued almost contemptuously:

"You can keep your Titanic, Hollywood," he sneered.

"King of the dark dank dare." He sipped his wine, swirled the glass and continued sarcastically:

"Your bright boy, Leonardo. Misnomer. The survivor speaks a part from a lesson of drama."

He stated as much about himself as Di Caprio.

"Others' experience is obnoxious to the individual with some sense of self," he observed solemnly.

"And how the professional actor is quite with himself is a fundamental interest to me."

"Heavy!" he concluded with a grin.

"Is that a concrete poem, not necessarily solid?" Again I had that humorous sense of being part of a 'piece', a living sculpture.

"To communicate more with the breath," he contemplated the implications.

"And as regards breath I assume as a creative person this intimacy should travel. The import of proximity, mindfully to embrace."

Suddenly he lightened:

"I've got three right feet and I dance on my left one Ma Tango. Thank you." He referred to the film, *Tango Lesson*, we had seen the previous night.

"I'm not disappointed by any bad news I've ever, ever, ever had," he reflected shaking his head.

"Kenneth Armitage described the physical world as either horizontally or vertically orientated, which I absorbed in my youth."

He paused and contemplated:

"Thought in sculpture and he is a fundamental thinker. I've made a success out of a Hare that thought, next to a thinker."

It was very rare for Barry to make or reveal anything about his process of work. He quickly concluded with a reference to John Cleese and Fawlty Towers:

"Stick with it Sybil."

"The intimacies of vehicles travelling this highway of life," he spoke softly, gently.

"In this out party, I guess we're acquainted," his voice suddenly sounded tired.

"Retreat from this light that illuminated it, this physical life."

There was a momentary silence, almost a premonition of death that Barry passed over.

"And regarding the water colourist," he began again getting up from his chair, "who knew Winston Churchill."

He began pacing:

"When I rebelled at the modesty of the fiscal price I volunteered more. She warned me, profligate." His eyes widened at the memory of this event.

"She accused me of doing so, an indulgence," then obscurely, "interpretation of prayer. And thus god bless us all," he lifted his glass and drank.

"With thanks, to another unread book, regardless of content." He said it contemptuously but continued gently.

"Thank you the Oscar winner Mr Niche."

"The commonality of civilianhood is the white juice I walk," he said this slowly and softly.

The humility of the statement brought tears to my eyes.

"Best wishes to Monsieur Rodin," he chirped up, "and Eric Fischl," he added, followed by the inevitable self-questioning:

"What conditions the art of keep praisers?"

He answered himself rhetorically.

"A sense of ceremony better than a destroyed novel as an approach to form?" It appeared like an oblique reference to Beckett and literature.

"My criticism is guarded. Deliver form," he demanded.

Suddenly he reverted back to one of his favourite subjects of respectful derision:

"The threshold of the digital era I break my nose on," he remarked.

"In the high jump one chooses to raise the bar. And the high jump is no medium for lawyers and professors. The civilians are not to be sucked into that art." He stated definitively.

"I do not fold any limb to my body." His voice drifted off, before he returned to the present.

"I'm a dancer," he said strongly, as a matter of fact.

"The novelist Beckett," he looked to his own future, perhaps, on the Emerald Isle.

"I'm not following his example in life. I'm not following that book in terms of goodwill, faith or zeitgeist."

He was definite in his resolve.

"I never had any argument with the interpretation of spirit, fallibly and faithfully."

He allowed for both sides of that treacherous kingdom. "Eat Jesus's knickers!"

He dramatically demanded standing up.

"Make a cake out of what remains," he exclaimed lifting his glass and draining it.

"The traveller in space? Been there, mind full of it," he wiggled his body at new age hippiedom and sat down again.

"Pay your bills and feed the hungry," he ordered.

"Placate the angry do better than no other," he pleaded.

"I'm not an anarchist," he revealed.

"Socialism to me is not politics, nor anarchy, more wishful thinking." The reality of his observations were glaringly obvious but he had not finished.

"And the responsibility refused by the power of no more, nor less, than the digital access."

The effrontery of such a situation almost bewildered him.

"Reducing communication to a dysfundament. Beyond the reduction of John Latham's dot!"[11]

---

11. 'Dysfundament' is a made up Barry word, a sort of equivalence of 'dysfunction', except 'fundamental' not 'functional'.

His indictment of society's direction became glaringly obvious. Suddenly he was up on his feet again:

"Yodel, scream! Nordic blast. Only the cold separates that anatomy of human frame. As to sculpture I complain," he rhymed.

"The mind is not naturally intelligent," he stated.

"Observation, by definition claims to reside in responsibility."

He listed some needs for the task:

"Self-consciousness, portrait, reflections, return, tick over. Evolve without the grace of tango," he finished with a flair.

"I love you Sally Potter! Today, the 10th of June 1998."

He slumped into a chair.

Suddenly he became pensive before continuing:

"Fear of lying is an interesting title."

"If in sculpture the figure has a front and back and sides."

"*Zen and the Art of Archery*. The author having no place in society addresses the points on an imaginary compass.[12]

"*Factor T* in Stefan Themerson's sense is really poignant. I'd have never been interested in John Latham or some of his contemporaries without my acquaintance and introduction to Stefan Themerson's *Factor T*.

Iconoclastically, I should be forgiven my continual reference to Alfred Jarry but he's an Icon – Gone!" he exclaimed.

"My role," he further explained, "is a matter of breath to the extreme but being a physical coward the pole is no frontier, nor the equator's drift."

He paused realising perhaps that the two bottles of Premier Cru had lifted us to another planet.

"The vulgar superstition that anomalies arrive from outer space,
one humours as a civilian.
No hoax, no fraud, fakes sued. A professional sculptor has no call.
The garden of life being a product and a little thought." His voice trailed off.

---

12. Eugen Herrigel, *Zen and the Art of Archery*, 1948

He stopped and smiled before he got up again and shook my hand gently.

It was a handshake that reminded me of his stone ground etching that I knew so well entitled *The Handshake* and featuring two Hares in such a pose.

He withdrew his arm and placed it behind his back, turned and shuffled out of the room.

"Eyes like a lilting leprechaun,
Moulding wax from old Byzantium
Bi-Actuals: emerald wisps will,
Delicate footprints, silver flair,
Marble membranes, bronzed infinite skill.
Grafting artefacts, altered states:
This, the heart laid bare,
One verse for a Leaping Hare."[13]

---

13. This poem I wrote about Barry after my first visit to his 'studio' in Ibiza 1988.

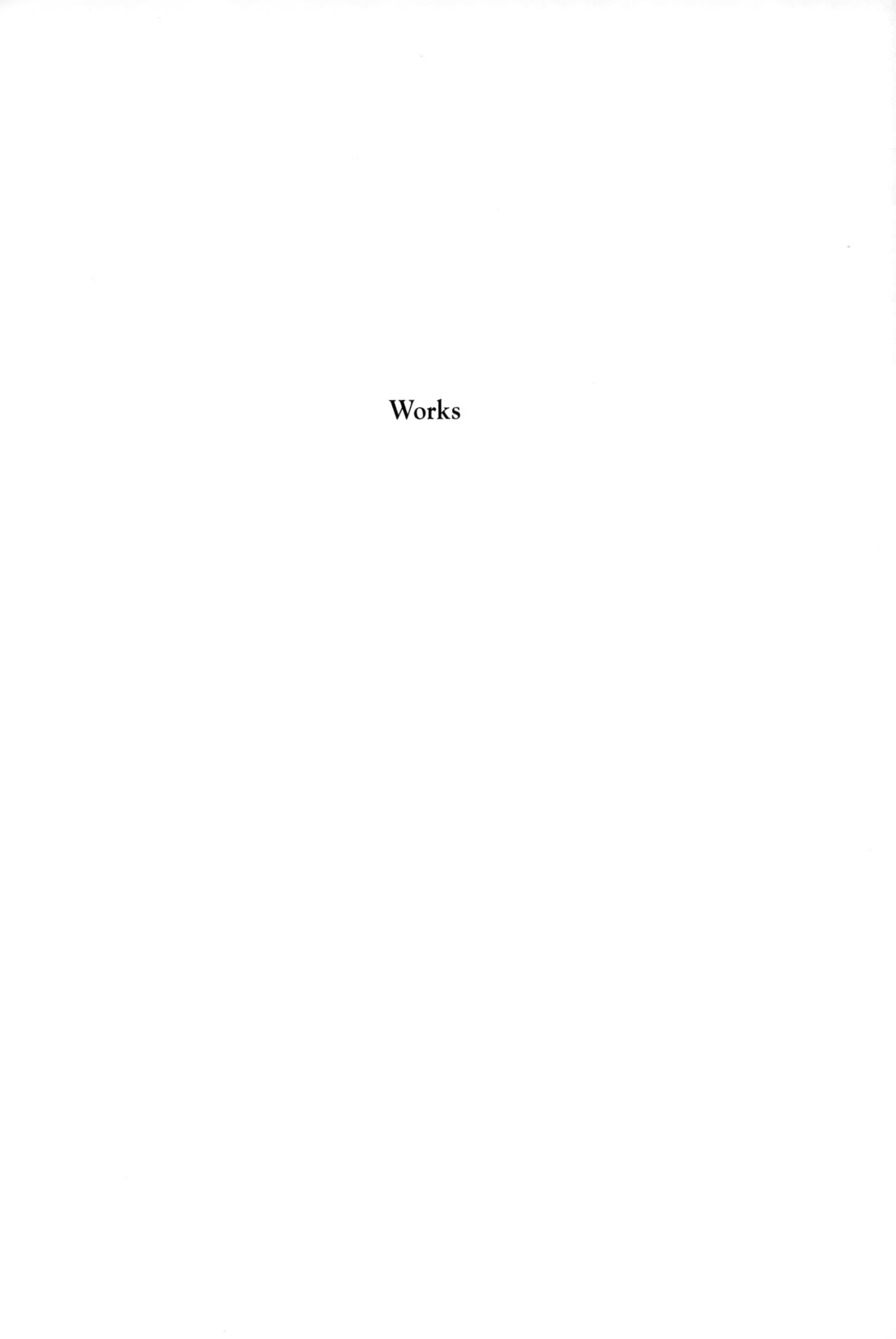

Works

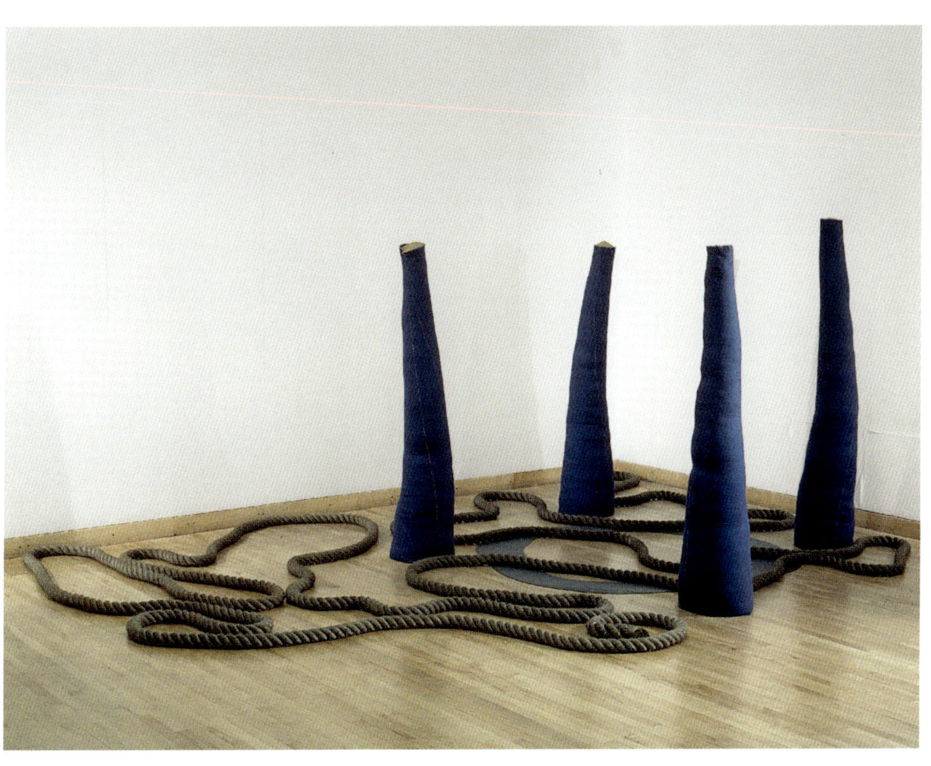

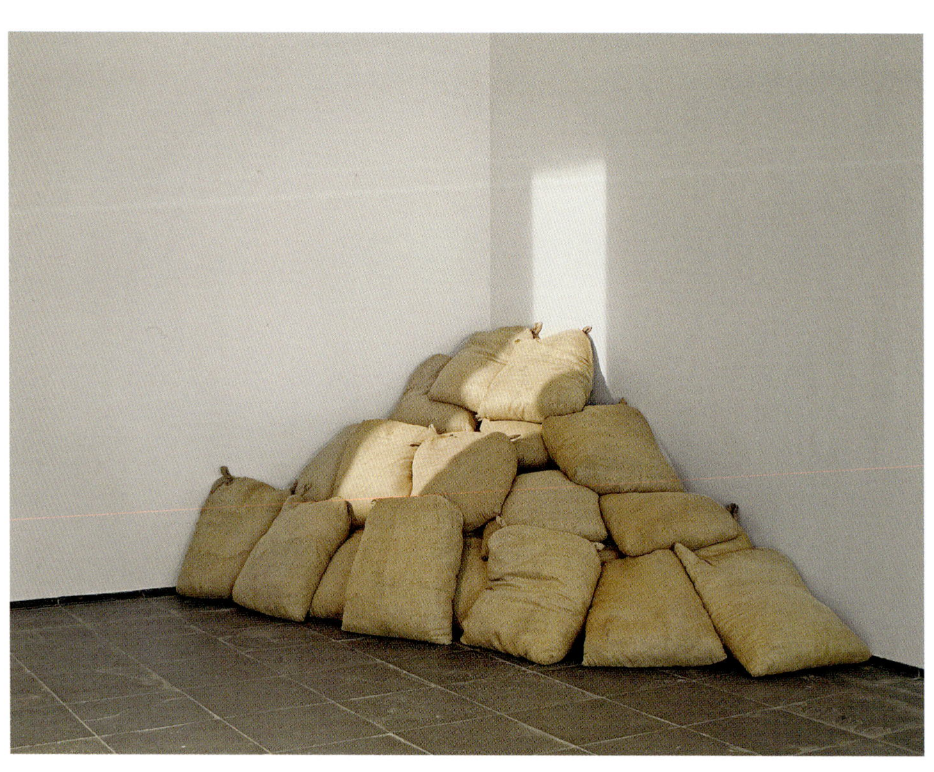

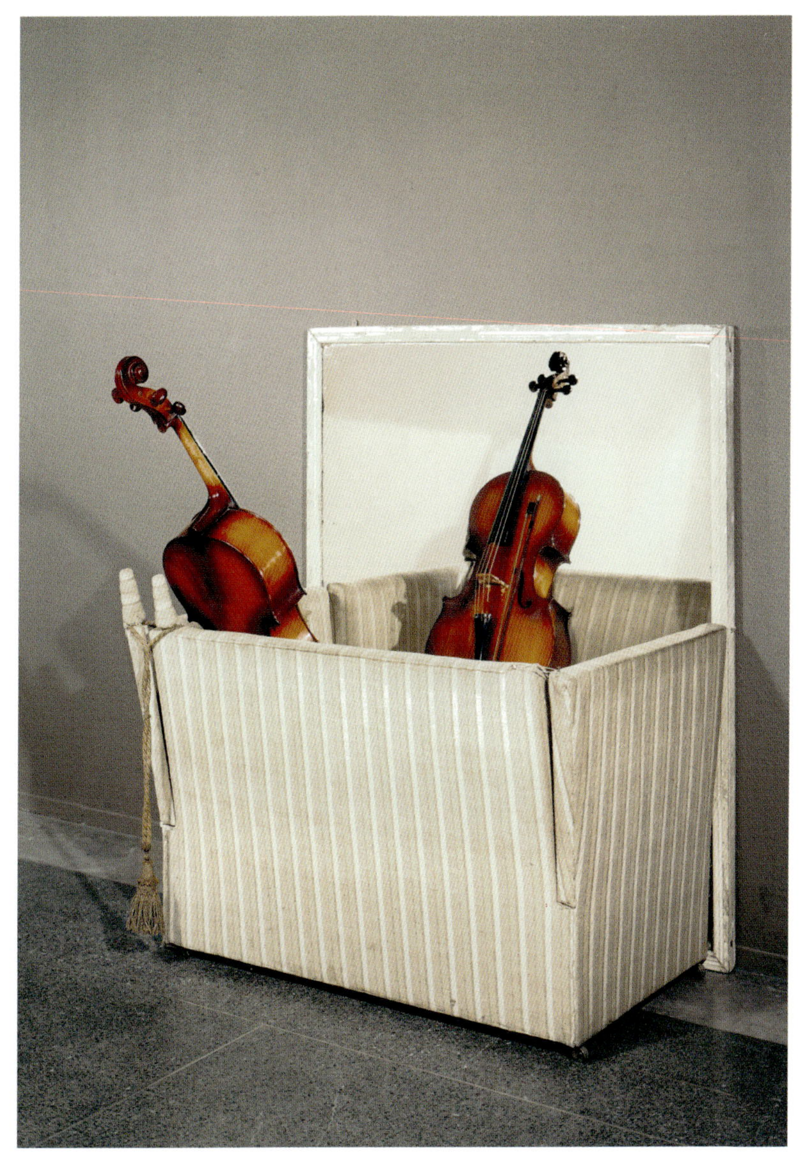

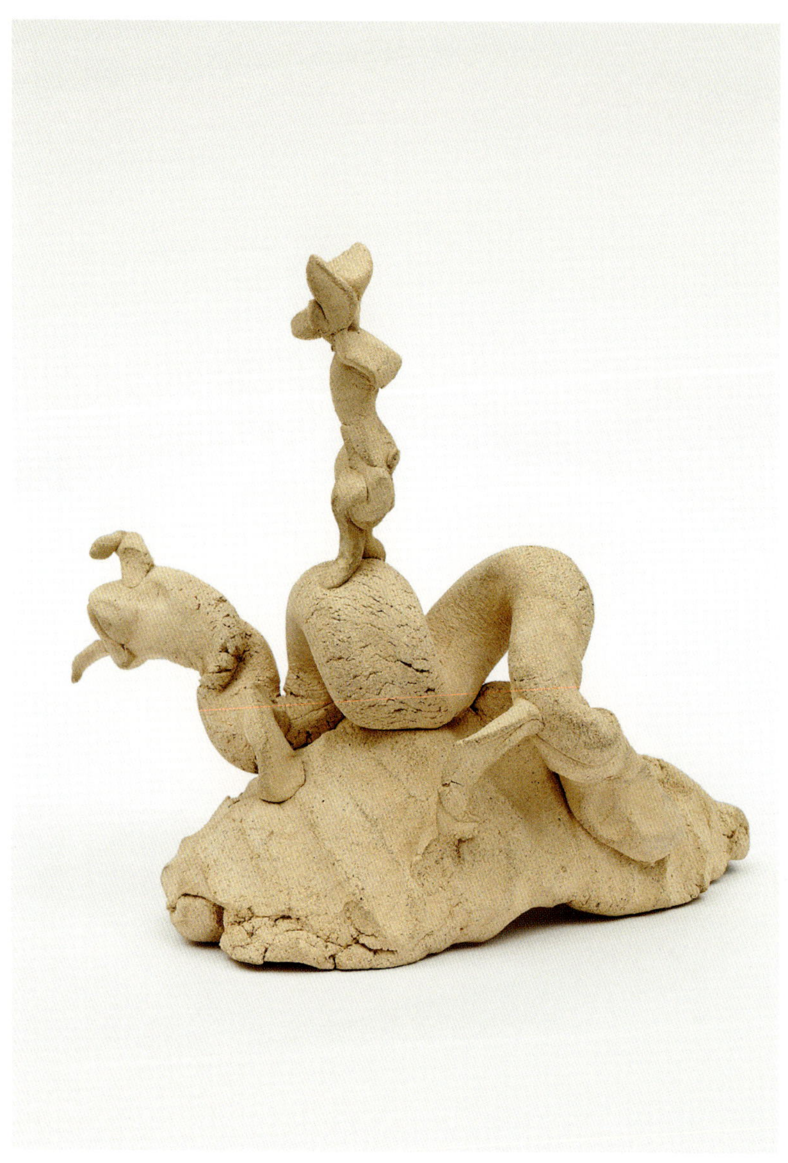

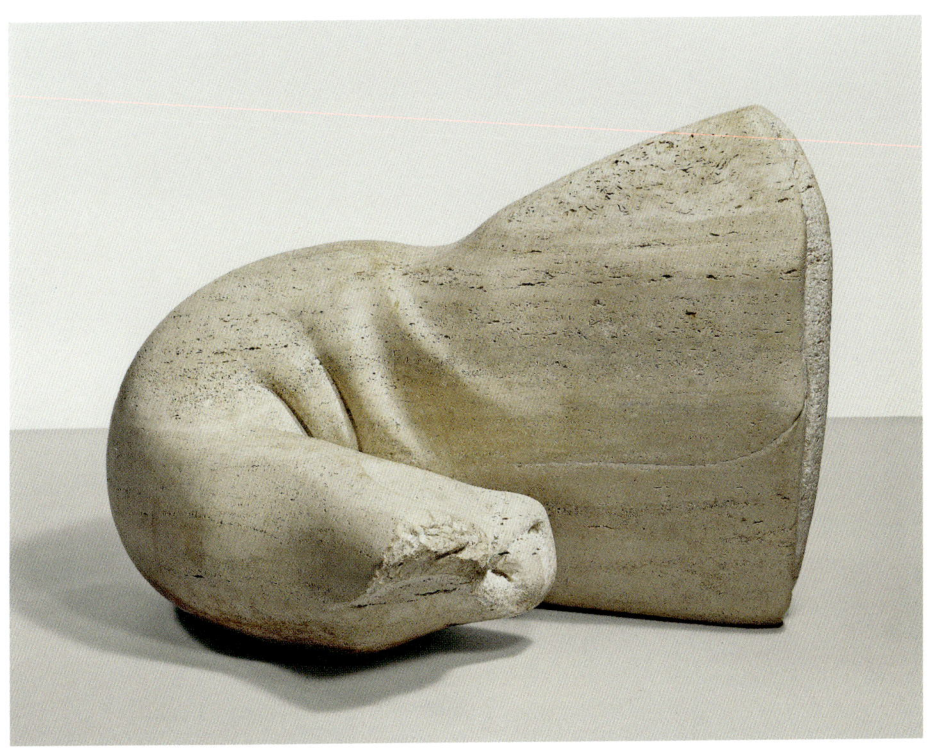

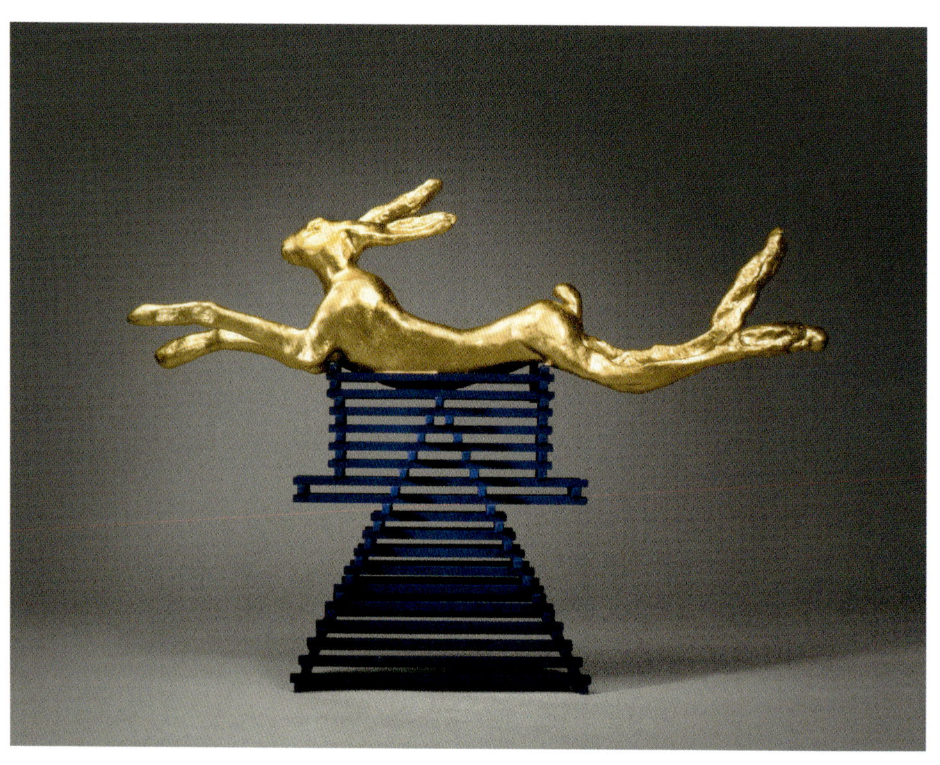

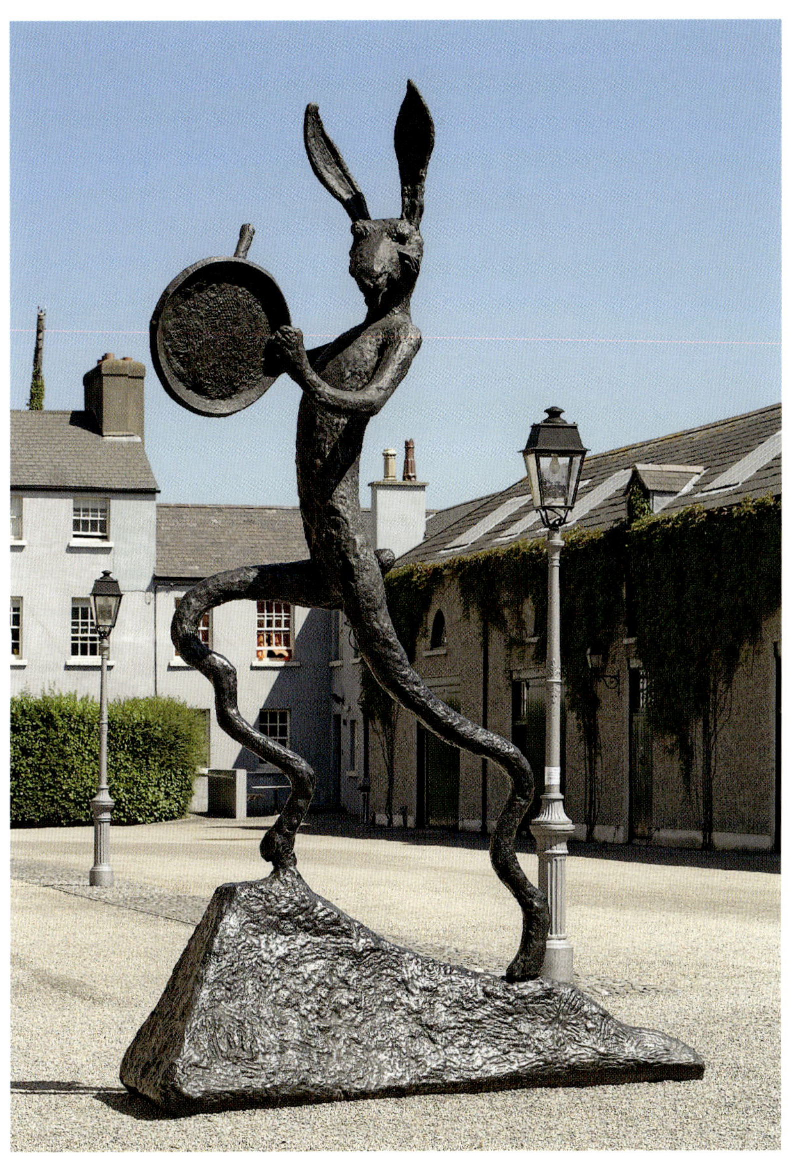

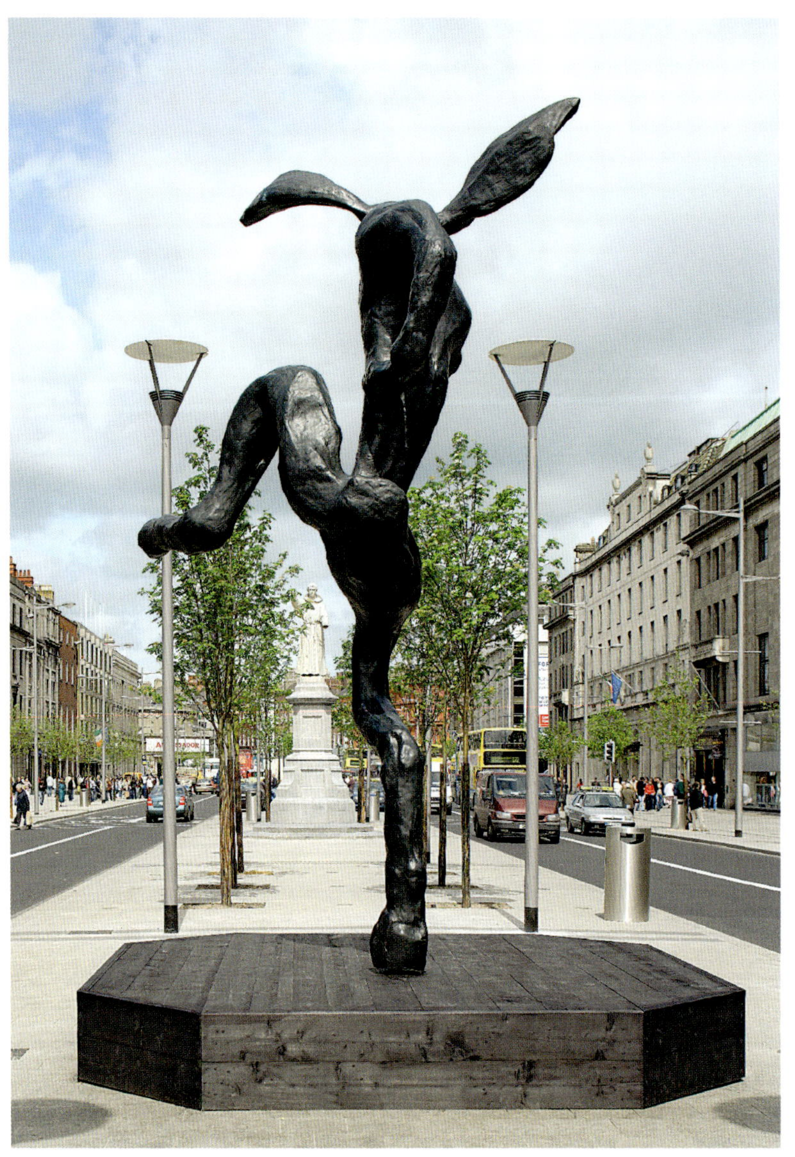

List of Illustrations

Appendix

About the Artist

Born in 1941, Barry Flanagan studied at the Birmingham College of Art and Crafts and St Martin's School of Art, London. He exhibited in numerous solo and group exhibitions internationally and in 1982 he represented Britain at the Venice Biennale. A major retrospective of his work was held at the Fundación "la Caixa", Madrid, in 1993, touring to the Musée des Beaux-Arts, Nantes, in 1994. In 1999 he had a solo exhibition at Galerie Xavier Hufkens in Brussels, followed by an exhibition at Tate Liverpool in 2000 and more recently at IMMA, 2006. His work is held in public collections worldwide and his bronze hares have been exhibited in many outdoor spaces, most notably on Park Avenue, New York, at Grant Park, Chicago, and most recently in O'Connell Street Dublin, a project curated by Dublin City Gallery the Hugh Lane in association with IMMA's retrospective exhibition in 2006.

Barry Flanagan's series of hare sculptures, which he began in the late 1970s, are among the most instantly recognisable artworks of the last twenty years. Playful, spontaneous and full of life, many show their subject engaged in human activities – dancing, playing musical instruments and sports and, more recently, using technology.

Flanagan saw the hare as a particularly suitable vehicle for these human endeavours and emotions, ". . . if you consider what conveys situation and meaning in a human figure, the range of expression is in fact more limited than the device of investing an animal – a hare especially – with the expressive attributes of a human being. The ears for instance are able to convey far more than a squint in the eye of a figure, or a grimace in the face of the model."

Inspired by his interest in the iconoclastic works of Alfred Jarry, the French poet, novelist, playwright and inventor of "pataphysics" (the science of imaginary solutions), Flanagan's earlier works from the 1960s and 1970s were regarded as extremely radical when first shown and continue to be so today. Many are of an ephemeral nature, such as *Light on light on sacks*, 1969, comprising a pile of hessian sacks illuminated by a beam of light. Works in stone and marble from the 1970s, including *The stone that covered the hole in the road (the skull)*, 1974, and *if marble smell of spring*, 1978, show a barely perceptible intervention by the artist. During the 1980s Flanagan also produced beautiful ceramic works and a series of marble sculptures, made in collaboration with Italian artisans from Pietrasanta.

About the Author

Robin Marchesi was born in Hampshire, England, 1951. He lived in Malta, Ireland and Nigeria while being educated at British boarding schools and later studied Humanities at London University followed by Literature and Politics at Oxford. Marchesi has published several books of poetry, including *A.B.C. Quest* (1991), *Kyoto Garden* (1996), *My Heart Is As* (2003) and also his early memoirs, *A Small Journal of Heroin Addiction* (2000).

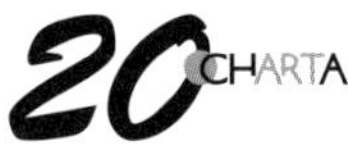

To find out more about Charta,
and to learn about our most recent
publications, visit

www.chartaartbooks.it

Printed in July 2011
by Bianca & Volta, Truccazzano (MI)
for Edizioni Charta